"When will it stop hurting?"

One man's journey through grief

GLENN CAMERON

Tellwell Talent
www.tellwell.ca

ISBN
978-0-2288-1630-0 (Hardcover)
978-0-2288-1629-4 (Paperback)
978-0-2288-1631-7 (eBook)

TABLE OF CONTENTS

ACKNOWLEDGEMENTS

The thought of writing a book, for me anyway, is somewhat terrifying. I enjoy my anonymity. Fame is something I have never desired. Not to imply the whole world is going to take notice when this book is published, but even if one person reads this book a piece of my privacy is gone forever. Friends and family will know my intimate feelings that were heretofore private. It is a daunting thought for me.

But in a way, I don't consider this my book. I recently listened to successful author Elizabeth Gilbert on a TED podcast. She shared a story of a book she began to write but for one reason or another she never completed the story. Years later she met an author who was writing a new book. As that author shared the details of her forthcoming book, Gilbert realized this was the story she had started years ago. The detail was startlingly similar. She expounded by clarifying that she believes all creative ideas are in the universe and looking for a way to come out through authors, poets, musicians; you get the idea. I subscribe deeply to her belief that all creativity comes from a supernatural source. I am not so concerned about what that source is. I have my own way of viewing the source, but I am very happy to allow another view that may be quite different from mine, to exist.

That being said, I feel my story was waiting to come out. Yes, it is using my own experience to deliver the message. But if I did not write this book, I feel the basic underlying message in my story would have found another author. I felt compelled to share my story.

Having no previous writing experience, at least in terms of publishing, I am grateful to have connected with Tellwell Publishing. Divinely transpired, I believe. My thanks to Maria for helping me start this process moving and giving me a comfort that I was making the correct decisions. Thank you to Gezel for managing the project. To Lara, who edited my book for content and grammar, I am humbled and filled with gratitude. Her attention to detail has made my book much more readable. Her insights and knowledge have added a polish to the final product. To Von, who created a cover that was just as I imagined, my gratitude for your creativity. To Von again, for taking a bunch of words in my manuscript and laying out those same words in a manner that makes it a book.

To Marty for his friendship and for helping me get a proper portrait photo so appease family members who were horrified at the iPhone selfie I originally sent Tellwell for my book cover.

To Crystle, my endless love, thank you for all you have taught me and continue to teach me. My grief has been intense but without having experienced your unconditional, uncompromising love I would never fully understand the depths of grief.

To Harley, our energetic six-pound Morkie terrier who snuggled beside me for hours, comforting me while I wrote the first drafts of this book. Her unconditional love helped me through many struggles over the past year.

To my family who have given feedback and supported me always, but especially over the last very challenging year. Valerie, Stephen, Megan, Kevin, Quinn, Nancy, and of course my mother. To Crystle's family who have supported me this past year as a brother. Special thanks to my nephew Chris for listening to me endlessly, which helped me formulate ideas that are in this book.

Thank you to the many friends who have supported me over this past year and given me the courage to keep going to finish this book.

Thank you to my friends and colleagues at Hospice Niagara. My volunteering provides me structure at a time when I need routine in my life. You have helped me beyond measure.

A sincere thanks to all who read this book. I hope it inspires you to defeat grief, if that is what brings you to these pages.

1

INTRODUCTION

On March 8, 2018, my world was shattered. Crystle, my wife of over 36 years passed away at the age of 58. She had been diagnosed with incurable brain cancer. It was an inevitable outcome that my mind had refused to acknowledge. Until it happened. We were entering our retirement years and looking forward to spending time with family and friends at our new home in Niagara.

If this book has spoken to you it is most likely that you, too, have suffered the loss of a loved one. In these pages I share my journey through grief in hopes that it may help you find some nugget of truth to help you defeat grief, for it is a terrible place to linger. I have learned two truths that I believe will be certainties for everyone taking the unwanted trip through the emotionally oppressive space of grief:

1 - No two journeys will be the same. I attended a grief therapy group just a few months after Crystle had passed away. It was a very neutral experience for me, but I know for certain it helped others. It does not mean either of us are somehow wrong, or not doing the things we should be doing to heal. There is no correct set of steps that one must take. Your intuition will tell you what the best choice is for you; trust your intuition.

2 - You will be a changed person. Whether for better or worse, I believe that no man or woman walks the path of grief and comes out the other side the same person. If you can defeat grief you will emerge stronger.

Crystle was, and for me, she will always be my soul mate. I do not use that term lightly. I recently penned in my journal that time is not mitigating our love to a warm memory. For me, it is still very much alive and growing stronger, as I move further past that dreadful day. Crystle and I spent much of our time together. It never really mattered to either one of us what we were doing as long as we were together. We could have been on vacation or snuggled together at home on the couch. We simply wanted to be together.

I was often fortunate to be her chauffeur. When the weather would turn bad, Crystle would turn on the charm and ask me to drive her to work. I am sure she felt that I was doing something special for her over and above the call of duty I had as her husband. But the truth is I cherished those fifteen minutes driving her to and from work. She was my rock. The more time I spent with her the more I felt grounded. And I confess I even looked forward to the times Crystle would *allow* me to go shopping with her. This was a privilege, for Crystle loved to shop alone. She puttered. She zigged and she zagged. She pondered. She picked things up and put them back. I am sure she was the focus of store security as they tried to figure out what this woman was going to do. It was relaxing for her to be alone. For me, it was like a treasure hunt. I would ask what she was looking for and go off on my own, eventually returning with items I thought may meet her approval. I knew that most of the time I would be taking things back to where I had found them, but every so often I would see a special look on her face. She would light up with approval. I was elated and that was my reward. I had found a treasure for my queen!

On Crystle's fifty-eighth birthday—yes, the exact day—she was diagnosed with glioblastoma multiforme. A terminal grade four brain tumour with a very grim diagnosis. Her diagnosis worsened when the surgeons informed us that they were unable to remove any of the tumour due to its location in her brain. I remember bursting into tears in the office of her family doctor as he read the results of the CT scan. When we arrived at the hospital that day, the hospital where Crystle had worked since we had moved to Niagara, she seemed calm. The director of her department brought down a single flower with a Happy Birthday greeting. Crystle was loved.

Less than eight months later she was gone. Taken away from friends and family. It was a gruelling time and an experience that I know many people have had to endure. The care Crystle received was full of compassion and for that I will be forever grateful. I don't believe I ever fully accepted the gravity of her diagnosis. Even while she was bedridden for the last two months of her life, I was still expecting a miracle. How could I not cling on to hope? I could not bear the thought of losing her.

When she passed away, I was broken in two.

I suppose shock came over me initially. For those last two months we were provided a shift nurse to sit with Crystle through the night so our family could get proper sleep and rest. With the assistance of personal service workers, our family provided Crystle's care through the end of her life, at home. I know this is not possible in many cases. I felt privileged to have been able to keep her home, but I could not have done so without the assistance of our children and community care nurses who visited Crystle every day, no matter the weather. And there was some treacherous weather. Crystle was not expected to survive the two months she was at home and eventually our shift nurse was taken from us. We were taking turns being with Crystle through the night. It was difficult but drew us even closer together as we cared for our beloved wife and mother. Then our wonderful palliative nurse from CCAC negotiated with the health care administration to provide a shift nurse to come in and be with Crystle so our family could get some much-needed rest. I fell asleep quickly that first night the nurse had returned. I had been in bed less than thirty minutes when the nurse came calling. I did not hear her, but my son was roused and came into my room to wake me. When he told me that the nurse had been calling me, I had a strong sense of what had happened. This is not unique: most of us have heard similar stories of knowing when a loved one has passed. I had much the same experience when my father passed away a few years earlier.

Crystle had passed. The love of my life was gone.

It took a year to convince myself that I had something valuable to share. I was inspired when I read a book titled, *Just Stay* [1], the story of a couple's journey with his diagnosis of pancreatic cancer. It is simply raw emotion of how they lived this period of their lives together, with family, and with their very special care team, until his passing. I have read many books over the past year and none spoke to me more profoundly than this book. It provided no specific advice, it simply shared their experience. In their words I found comfort. As I read their story, I was able to find pieces of their journey that helped me reconcile the decisions I had made for Crystle during her illness. It was hard to avoid judging myself and second-guessing the choices I had made. Their story didn't discuss the aftermath of grief, but it allowed me to forgive myself, and perhaps more importantly know that every decision I made was made out of pure love for Crystle.

My story is about grief. It is my personal experience as I worked through the pain I felt in losing Crystle. Grief is a harsh emotion that overcame me in ways I could never have imagined. I faced anger, jealousy, guilt, hopelessness and aloneness. I confess my mind even wandered into the realm of suicide. In the end, I determined life was very much worth living.

---

1   Jennifer Fazakerley, Helen Butlin-Butler, and Grace Bradish, Just Stay--: a couple's last journey together, (Toronto, 2012),

I am not a trained therapist, counsellor, or medical practitioner. My undergraduate degree is in business and I have been an IT professional for most of my career. I kept asking myself, "What can I offer people? What is different about my story?"

Experience is what I have to offer. The real-life experiences in *Just Stay* helped me, so maybe my story can help others, too. I have walked the dark path of grief and emerged into the daylight. The sun looks different now but there is sunshine and for that I am grateful. I don't think anyone ever completely recovers from loss of a loved one, but you can defeat the grief.

This book is not a guide through grief. There will be no *ten steps* to recovery. I do not intend to imply that books offering advice and specific steps to overcoming grief are not important. There are many books offering *solutions* to grief. I recommend anyone going through grief read at least one of these books. I have read many books over the past year relating to grief and each one has given me a small piece of my own personal puzzle. Each time I read a book, some piece would connect with me and slowly I began to get the upper hand on my own grief.

The grief group I attended after Crystle passed allowed me to meet fellow travellers on the road of grief. I was doing reasonably well, at least as I judged myself. About halfway through the eight-week session, one of the members of our group asked the facilitator a question: "When will it stop hurting?" The question pierced through me. If ever I experienced compassion it was at that moment. This member of our group had lost a spouse, too, about the same time as Crystle had passed. I had pondered the very same question myself. But my perspective was different. It was then I realized how unique the process of working through grief is for each of us. This member of our group was lost in grief and the question was framed in the hope that if a certain amount of time passed, the hurt, too, would pass. The truth is there is no time frame by which you should *feel better.* I have met others who tried to wait out grief, but grief seems to have infinite patience. It won't simply go away unless we make it go away.

My deepest hope in sharing my story is that some of what I write will be a help, in some small way, so that others can use a part of my path through grief to find their own unique way to healing.

2

GRIEF

I don't sigh much anymore. But occasionally one sneaks out. It has been almost a year, as I write this, since Crystle passed. Now when I sigh it comes over me at the most unexpected times, often triggered by a memory that could be deemed insignificant to the casual observer. I was in a Walmart store one day when suddenly tears started pouring down my face. I had walked into an aisle that sparked a memory. We had wandered apart from each other that day and as I came into this very aisle in which I was now standing, I saw Crystle at the far end. I remembered such a feeling of love for her, smattered with relief and joy at finding her wandering about as if without a care. For me, these memories strike a chord deep within my soul. For a brief moment I feel like I am being pulled into the past, as if I am being moved through some beam of light that we might find in a science fiction novel. For that brief period of time I have been transported back to those early days just after Crystle left us. The memory is so fresh in that moment I feel like I can reach out and touch her. It is fleeting, thankfully, and just as quickly I am moved, seemingly at the speed of light, back to the present moment.

What are these sighs? I wondered to myself in those early days of grief. They began almost immediately after Crystle passed and at first, they came frequently. The Oxford dictionary defines a sigh as "to emit a long, deep, audible breath expressing sadness, relief, tiredness, or a similar feeling."

These sighs became a hallmark in the early days of my grief.

In the first month after her passing the sighs seemed to come like waves on the shore. Relentless, they continued their march. Defying logic, each sigh crashed into the present moment before any thought of Crystle had a chance to come into my mind. They would bubble up and come out of me with little warning, as if to taunt me. They were a constant reminder that Crystle was no longer with me. But with each sigh came some mysterious relief, even if just for a few moments, and that was a welcome reprieve. Perhaps, I pondered, they were the result of some internal pressure relief system much like you would see when steam is released from a boiler. If there is no way to release pressure in that boiler, it will simply explode at some point. I learned to accept them as a coping mechanism. But every sigh reminded me of Crystle, and I knew that my relief would be short-lived. I knew that very soon the knots would return to tie up my stomach into the aching that had become my constant companion.

I had become an unwilling participant in a journey through grief, thrust into a dark forest that I had no choice but to find my way out of or I could be lost forever. I thought I knew what grief was like and that I understood its grip. For if you had asked me even one day before Crystle passed I would have told you that I was fully aware of grief and I was ready to take it on.

Oh, was I wrong!

I searched the internet for the word *grief* and found definitions at great length that loosely describe grief as an emotional response to loss. That loss may not only be due to the death of a loved one, it can also be the end of a relationship, and while I have never experienced loss due to a broken relationship, to me it seems the grief could be just as intense as it would in death. If a person you have loved is no longer in your life, what does it matter the cause?

Why am I elaborating on the definition of grief? To define the narrow scope of my journey and hence this book. Since I am sharing my personal story, this book will discuss grief as it relates to the loss of a loved one, and more specifically, the loss of a spouse or life partner. I can only share what I know from personal experience. However, I suspect the shroud of grief and its terrible pangs are shared by each of us no matter whence it has come upon us.

That being said, I do hypothesize that not all grief is the same. And I most certainly do not feel we all experience grief in the same way. But what I have discovered is that to make such a statement is somewhat taboo. In my walk with grief, it seemed to me, as I began my attempt to try to understand what grief was, that I was being led to believe that all grief is homogenous. That was simply not my experience, and I quickly found myself becoming very guarded in sharing my true thoughts. I felt oddly pressured to be politically correct by saying that we all experience grief at the same level. It became a common theme provided to me by authors and speakers who ostensibly preferred tiptoeing around the subject. So, I began to tiptoe with them.

To make such a bold statement may seem pious. But my belief, again, comes from my own experience. I lost my father just twenty months before my wife passed away. I love my dad dearly. I have such fond memories with him. He was a pastor in an evangelical denomination. He excelled in his profession and I am very proud to say he is my father. He didn't just preach hell, fire and brimstone; he ministered to people in their everyday lives. He went into their kitchens when they hurt. Visited them in the hospital when they were sick. He cared for the elderly through regular visitation. People joked with him, telling him he was well paid for only working one day a week. I knew they were joking, but it still bothered me. I saw the truth, that his vocation was truly seven days a week. He was a very busy man, yet he always made time for his family. When he was a teenager, my dad was a pitcher for the baseball team at his school. I remember playing catch with him in the backyard and still have vivid pictures in my mind of him showing me how to throw a curveball. I felt like I had been given a secret that no other boy knew. In the wintertime, Dad would take my friends and me out onto the rural roads where there was no traffic and tow us on toboggans behind the car. Can you imagine a father dragging children behind a moving vehicle today? I am glad I am a product of the sixties and seventies. Then there is the time he bought me a ten-speed bicycle when I know he didn't have the money. I still wonder today how he did it. I felt safe. I felt loved. When he passed away, I shed tears and I was sad. But the truth is my life returned to normal very quickly. In July 2016, the passing of my father became my reference for what grief was all about. I would have said that in grief you are sad for a few weeks and then life goes on. Then Crystle passed, and I had an entirely new perspective on grief. Not all grief is the same.

Why does it matter? Why am I making such a kerfuffle about comparing grief? I think it is important because our very human nature compels us to compare everything, and in grief, especially, that is very dangerous. I am so grateful I have never lost a child and since I have never experienced the pain of losing a child, how can I make a judgment that my grief, in losing a spouse, is more or less severe? Or even more absurd, how can I say it is the same? How can I make a judgment of a man sitting next to me who has just lost his wife? I cannot, nor should I try to do so. But I am confident in saying his grief is different than mine. His journey will be unique from my experience with grief. He may take longer to reach a point where grief no longer consumes him, or he may reach that plateau very quickly. It does not mean he has dealt with his grief any better or worse than I may have done. He has simply followed his own path in grief and dealt with it as best he knew how.

I do not mean to be repetitive, but I consider this to be a true nugget of wisdom that was so valuable in helping me heal from my grief. Once I realized that my journey was my own, and that I did not have to compare myself to anyone else, or follow any specific outline for defeating grief, I gained a freedom that propelled me forward in overcoming grief.

So how did grief change for me when Crystle passed away?

For the first week after she passed, our home was busy. It was filled with family as we prepared a celebration of life for Crystle. It was a good distraction, if I can use that expression. But at the same time, I was succumbing to a myriad of negative emotions.

I was becoming very angry. Why me? Or more importantly, why Crystle? Surely there was no more loving or gentler woman on this earth than Crystle. I was becoming angry with a God that I was not even sure existed. I lashed out at God anyway. I cursed him and told him he should have taken me. I told God that Crystle's passing only proved what I had suspected: He was not real. "God is a fairytale," I thought to myself, as if trying to goad Him into showing himself to me. My anger spilled over to others. I became angry with her physicians and the decisions they made for her medications and for her care. I lashed out at the insurance company as I began the process of making a claim. I was angry that I even had to endure this process. My anger would build until my emotions poured out in tears of hopelessness. The first time I called the insurance company I had to hang up because I was sobbing so hard, I could not make any intelligent sounds come from my being.

Then there was jealousy. I remember watching a couple walking hand in hand through the outlet mall, a place I would only ever be with Crystle. I wanted to walk up to them and shout, "Hey, my wife was taken from me. Do you know that?" I wanted everyone to feel sorry for me. Especially the happy couple! I wanted everyone to know my pain. If I could not have my wife to hold my hand, then everyone should share in my sadness.

I felt guilty. Why had I not had these intense feelings of grief when my father passed away? Did I not love him enough? Why had I not realized how my mother was hurting? Surely, she had faced the same pain when the live of her life left us. And to compound all my emotions, I felt guilty about my jealousy and anger.

This cocktail of emotions was bottled up inside of me. No wonder the sighs erupted from my soul so frequently during this time. I thought no one knew how I was feeling in those early days of grief. And I think it's probably fair to say that there were some who do not know how I was feeling. But many understood. Many have walked in grief.

By the time Crystle's celebration of life was over I just wanted to be alone. I asked our children to leave me alone for a while. No phone calls. No texts. No contact. I knew I had to face this beast—grief—on my own terms. I didn't know it then, but I would need the help and support of friends and family more than I ever could have imagined. But I was determined to start the fight on my own.

Grief, for me, was oppressive. It was like wearing clothing fabricated from lead. My steps were heavy and slow. I felt as if my stomach had been tied into a knot and then knotted again. A dull ache spread throughout my entire body. It seemed that truly every fibre in my body was screaming in pain. It was difficult for me to put a thought together. In the morning I would come downstairs and make a cup of coffee. Then I would just stand there. Sometimes literally standing for ten or fifteen minutes, just staring into space, and by the time I took that first sip of coffee it had become lukewarm.

There was no thought process, my mind was grappling with the reality of Crystle's death and trying to find a way out. For these few moments in the morning, emotions seemed to drain out of me, and I just stood there with the cold of the kitchen tile against my feet. I was not angry, or sad, or lonely. I was just empty, devoid of all feelings, consumed in my grief.

Sleep became altered for me. I have always joked with anyone who cared to listen that I had a PhD in sleep. "Stand me in a corner and I will be fine," I would quip. Now, my nights were restless. I would drift in and out of sleep with the same story repeating over and over. How can I change the ending of this story? My mind still refusing to accept her death, I would play out scenario after scenario. I would start to slip away into sleep as my mind continued to review the steps I could take in hopes of a different outcome. Then reality would invade my consciousness like a bell ringing beside my head.

"She is gone. She is gone!" shouted that damn voice in my head.

This scene repeated itself over and over until I fell into sleep from exhaustion. Sleep, when it finally overtook me, was like a gift from heaven. For in those precious few hours I was free of grief. But as soon as I awakened, it all started again. It was torture.

There never seemed to be any tears in my restless sleep. But that was not the case once I was fully awake. Tears poured from me to the point I wondered how I could not be dehydrated. Coffee and tears are not a good combination for anyone looking to be hydrated. In defence of my tears, I will say that I welcomed them. I would sit with pictures of Crystle and allow the memories to cascade over me. So many tears would flow. I have learned through this journey that science explains that when we cry emotional tears, we release chemicals that help ward off stress. I came to rely on those times when I would just sit and cry, and I eventually stopped feeling like this was somehow a sign of weakness. It became a time of release and refreshment.

There is a parable telling of a woman who sought help of a sage after the death of her child. She was told to seek out and find a mustard seed from a family that had never known sorrow to release her from her grief. The story says she travelled all over the world and while she did not find the mustard seed, she found understanding, compassion, and friendship. This was another step in my journey through grief. Another blow delivered to the beast.

When I realized that many of the people I encountered every day have also experienced the pain and sorrow of grief, it was cathartic. Even the happy couple walking hand in hand had probably experienced loss. I was not alone. No matter how far and wide I may search, I, too, would never find the mustard seed of a family without sorrow. But I did find compassion, caring, and love.

What follows in the forthcoming chapters is the story of my journey through grief. Again, I hope that everyone who reads my story will find that some small portion of it may help them as they make their way on their own journey through grief.

Here is my story.

3

PHOTOGRAPH

The power of a photograph has been extolled by songwriters, bards, and storytellers for eons. Many have used the well-known cliché, "a picture is worth a thousand words," as their inspiration. I am going to show you a picture of a man—me, of course. It's an imaginary picture but it is clear in my mind. I hope you can see it too, in your mind's eye. Let me tell you what I see, but I may need more than a thousand words.

This picture was taken the morning after Crystle passed. Her body still rests in our home, but I cannot bring myself to sit with her. It's not her, anyway, just an empty body. I am sitting in the kitchen trying to be normal in front of my family, but inside I am numb.

"When will it stop hurting?"

Click.

The picture captures my face and if you look deeply you will find a man who has lost hope in life. If you look more carefully, you can see his journey into hopelessness, from birth to the moment the picture was snapped.

I was born with a cleft palate and lip. And to make life a bit more challenging for my mother, I was a breech birth. As a child, I was teased a lot about my physical deformity. I don't recall the moment I became aware that I was *different* from other children. As children often do, when they see something that makes you different from everyone else you become a magnet for hurtful words. What made me different? My nose was crooked, kind of pushed in on the left side, and I had a scar running from my left nostril to my upper lip. I feel fortunate because the surgeon who repaired my cleft palate and lip performed his work so well that I believe his hands must have been guided by God. My scars are scarcely visible today and I have no speech impediment that often results from having a cleft palate.

In childhood, even my closest friends would sometimes turn to teasing me, although not very often. Those moments hurt more than the laughter from children I barely knew at all. I internalized the hurt. Sometimes

I would try to defend myself but that seemed only to make matters worse. Like wild animals smelling blood, sensing they had made me angry or sad or caused any sort of reaction only made the taunting worsen. Those experiences made me fiercely independent. I relied only on myself because my trust in others had disintegrated. Even today, trusting others is a challenge that I work to overcome. Ultimately, it created emotional walls in me that I put up as barriers and I seldom let anyone inside.

I grew up on the east coast of Canada in the home of an evangelical pastor. Our family was borderline poverty level, I think, but it didn't feel that way to me. My mother was an expert at putting together wonderful meals on a budget. We always had plenty of food and never went hungry. I always had trendy clothing to wear. The people in the local church were very generous to our family. Our home was always clean through the hard work of my mother. It was full of love and caring for each other, and for others.

My grandfather had a cottage on the Saint John River, so we were able to spend a few weeks every summer going to the beach and enjoying rural New Brunswick. Days at the cottage were carefree. Swimming with friends at the local beach for hours. Sunscreen was unheard of; instead, Noxzema cream was used to soothe the inevitable sunburn. There was a tire swing in front of our cottage that swung out over bushes that sloped away from me, so that at the full extension of the swing I seemed to be flying through the air. I remember the sound of the air whooshing in my ears. As the swing stopped at its full extension before beginning its return to the launching point, there was that split second of silence before the wind was in my ears again. That moment of silence was in some strange way a friend. There was a trust. It never let me down. It was always there at the end of each swing outward. It was a carefree time providing some of the best memories from my childhood.

We took family vacations to Maine and New Hampshire, and when I was four years old, we drove to Niagara Falls. Family was very important to my parents. My childhood home was a safe haven, which was so important in giving me the strength I have even today. Despite our modest family income, my childhood life never seemed to be lacking adventure.

I always had friends to play with and was active in sports, playing organized baseball and hockey. With my pals we would play any sport available to us: football, soccer, golf, basketball, road hockey. We built forts made from scrap wood that we had dragged from all over town. I was always on the go. I loved to ride my bike and knew every street and alley in town. For the most part I had a happy childhood, even if occasionally marred by teasing.

I did well in school. I found learning easy, which may have been a double-edged sword. As I progressed through high school, I found myself selecting courses based on doing the least amount of work for the best grade. I suppose my parents never intervened because I could always eke out a good grade. I tend to think of myself as an introvert, yet I love social environments. Is there such a thing as a social introvert? If there is, that's me! I was never involved in many extracurricular activities in school, especially once I reached high school. A big part of that was my penchant for money. Money gave me the independence that I desired. Not an independence from my family but rather a feeling of security in myself.

When I was twelve, I took a paper route. My first job. I was thrilled to be earning my own income. It was the worst paper route in town because it required walking the most distance and had the fewest customers. I didn't care. I was making money. Soon I was working in other jobs after school, so I always had money in my pocket. One of the more interesting jobs I had was working for a heating wholesaler. I worked two days a week after school. Most of the time I was sorting through a large box of parts and sorting them into gear assemblies of two unique sizes. My workspace was a large cardboard box turned upside down. Once I had ten of each size, I taped them into a bundle. At the end of my shift I would take the results of my work upstairs where they would be used for rebuilding oil pumps used in furnaces.

I was diligent in my work and the men were always friendly. In hindsight, I am guessing they were happy because I was doing a dreadfully boring job that one of them had to do before I showed up at their door. The shipper/receiver for the company was a local hockey hero on the Junior B hockey team. Rumour was that he had been invited to a few NHL training camps but that is where his professional hockey career ended, as far as I know. Even so, I was star-struck. I had watched Jim play hockey at many games in the local arena. I was even more thrilled when he befriended me. That meant when no one was looking I got to enjoy (so I thought) activities that were fun. Jim was happy to let me drive the forklift to move things around the warehouse. Not often—I imagine they were times when it was convenient for Jim to do so. My training was five minutes with Jim standing beside me while I put a pallet on the warehouse racks and then retrieved it again. I guess we both figured if I could do it once that should be enough training. Thankfully, there are no tragedies for me to share as a result of my forklift driving. But perhaps one of my favourite things to do was destroy products that had been returned under warranty. Rather than return them to the manufacturer they gave me a sledgehammer to smash heating and electrical parts into pieces. To this day I am not certain why we were destroying these parts—I assume it was easier than returning them to the manufacturers. Anyway, it was fun for a fourteen-year-old boy!

My parents were very open-minded in terms of their religion and beliefs. For both my sister and me that meant that when we reached the age of sixteen, we were free to make our own choice about attending church. I continued to attend out of respect for my parents. But by the time I was sixteen, I felt organized religion was not for me. I just went through the motions of attending church. I took religion very seriously, even if it was of little interest to me. I was often one of the few who would not take communion when it was offered on Sunday. Not in defiance; no, very much the opposite, I refused communion out of respect for the doctrine of the church in which my father was a pastor. I felt that taking communion as a non-believer was blasphemous to God and bringing damnation to myself. Even if I was not sure God was real.

When I turned eighteen, I felt I was ready to experience life.

You could say that I am a bit of an adrenalin junkie, always looking to go faster or jump off something higher. I broke both arms in my teens (not at the same time). And in gym I tripped and fell as we chased each other before a class, breaking a front tooth that the orthodontist had just spent two years straightening. So, when I turned eighteen and the opportunity came to attend technical school in Toronto, I packed my bags and headed out. My mother was not well at the time and to this day she still reminds me that I left home while she was ill. I believe she has forgiven me—well, almost.

I don't believe in coincidence, so I will have to say that a higher power intervened in my move to Toronto. I was looking to "sow my wild oats," but instead I ended up in the home of a Christian couple. I can never forget that snowy evening when my flight landed in Toronto. I had never met Ed so to find each other he was carrying a coil of yellow rope. It was 1979. I have to laugh in hindsight because I can only imagine the commotion that would arise today if someone were to walk into a major airport carrying a coil of yellow rope? SWAT teams would be engaged.

Ed and Mabel never pushed me to go to church with them, but I got along very well with them and it just seemed like the civil thing to do. Before I knew it, I was back in church every Sunday. I became active in church and was a charter member and secretary of the board of a brand-new church in North Toronto. I was embracing religion—again. And that is where I met Crystle. A blind date organized by her sister who had a well-deserved reputation as Cupid's assistant, and whom I had gotten to know through attending church. The blind date led to more dates and within a few years we decided to spend our lives together. We were married young. I was a month away from turning twenty-one and Crystle was twenty-two. Family also came early. We had two children by the time I turned twenty-seven.

As we moved into our mid-thirties, church was fading as a part of our life. Events happened that made me wonder about God. I was browsing in a bookstore one day and I came across a book titled *Godless*. I have no idea why I came across this book, but remember: I don't believe in coincidence. It is the story of its author, Dan Barker. He had grown up much like me except he had become a pastor. He shares his story of how he lost his faith and became an atheist. While I vibrated with what he wrote in his book, I was not ready to deny the existence of God. I was, however, okay thinking that I did not need to believe in God unless he showed himself to me. It took me another five years to be comfortable in saying there was no God—at least, no

God of which I could find any evidence. By my early forties I was fully agnostic and quietly went about my non-believing. Crystle and I had conversations about church and religion over the years. There was never any disagreement but we both saw things differently. What was clear was that I had embraced agnosticism more fully than had she.

Our lives revolved around our children, and my work in information technology took me away on many Sundays, the time when changes and updates were often scheduled in corporate data centres. Church became less and less a factor in our lives. Neither of us were seeking to make any bold statements to our families and friends. We loved our families and respected their beliefs. I became very comfortable with my agnosticism as the years passed. I am not fully certain how Crystle felt and I wish we had discussed the topic more deeply than we had. I believe Crystle never gave up her belief in God but struggled with how to relate that within the structure of organized religion. As my work took me away on many Sundays, Crystle quietly went about life without the church and didn't seem too bothered by that eventuality.

My life was, for the most part, trouble-free. Even with my cleft palate, I felt I had no serious emotional scars. Perhaps my path through life had made me very naïve. I was married young to the love of my life. This is not to say we didn't have a few bumps on the road of our marriage, for we certainly did. But after thirty-six years of marriage I loved Crystle more than ever. Reflecting back, it bothers me that I had never stopped to consider the feelings of those who had never been married or faced loneliness in unhappy marriages. An image comes to my mind now in later days. An image of a person watching me holding Crystle's hand as we walked together through an outlet mall. That person is looking at me and is running up to me to say—well, you probably know what they would say. I know that I do, now that I have become that person.

I lived in my own little bubble. I didn't know what compassion really meant. Oh sure, I could speak the word, but I was not compassionate. I was caring and helped others, but compassion escaped me. I am not sure I could have even empathized with others, much less shown compassion. True compassion, I would have thought, must surely be for men like my father. I am not trying to be self-deprecating; it is sadly the fact of who I was, and to a larger extent, a reflection of our society. We are taught to strive for a happy marriage with happy children. To have a good job, a nice car, a beautiful home, and take vacations every year. We are not taught to look out for those among us who are hurting. I was simply a product of our culture.

So at the very moment Crystle passed, my path in life resulted in me being a man with no faith. No belief in an afterlife. My deep agnosticism left me without any hope. I didn't for a moment consider my religious roots as an outlet for comfort; in fact, I shunned religion. I would have quite possibly reacted in anger had someone other than family suggested prayer. I didn't want or need any prayers. Once Crystle's body was gone, the urn containing her ashes was all that I had. I believed Crystle was gone forever. I clung to the urn in desperation and never thought of burying those precious ashes in the first weeks after Crystle left us.

It was a perfect storm. I was thrust into a world of grief for which I was not prepared, with no beliefs to support me, and therefore no hope in my future.

It has been over a year now. My photograph has been lying on the shelf. You can pick it up and blow from it the dust that has collected. At first you may not discern it was snapped just a few moments after the love of my life had died. Would you be able to see the hurt I was feeling? Could you see the hopelessness in my eyes? Not likely unless you really knew me. Perhaps if you had the photo album of my life you might notice something wasn't right with my smile. Maybe my shoulders were slouching. Whether the observer could see it or not, my photograph that day showed a man who was forever changed. A man who felt he had no hope. I am reminded of two lines I once read from a short verse, author unknown:

Our tomorrow never came,
Nothing in my life is the same.

4

FIRST STEPS

One night as I lay sleeping, I had a vision in a dream. It was not long after Crystle passed. It created a vivid image for me, an image that represents those of us who are facing grief. There is a large open field covered in beautiful flowers of many colours and varieties. Crystle loved flowers and I came to enjoy them too, through her passion. They remind me of her. I feel happy in this place. The grass is lush and green—it feels like velvet on my bare feet. The sun shines brightly and there is a warm gentle breeze on my face. The breeze reminds me of childhood, caressing me with memories of those carefree days on my tire swing.

But then my eyes are drawn to the edge of that field. There awaits a dense forest. I interpreted the field to represent my life, filled with beauty and happiness. But as we lose our loved one, each of us must walk up to the edge of the forest leaving the beautiful meadow behind. It is dark and foreboding in the forest. The beauty of the field is fading as I am unable to prevent my focus from shifting to the forest. I look at the others who have come to the edge of the forest with me, having, too, lost a loved one. There are many of us here at this moment. The forest facing me appears to be an impenetrable tangle of trees and underbrush. The forest represents the grief I must confront. Again, I look over each shoulder at the people on either side of me, and then, as if in some crazy concerted effort, each of us enters the forest at the same time but from a different place. Once we have been swallowed up into its darkness, we must each find our own path through. We can try to help each other but the dense forest makes each of us feel alone. We forget about each other, neither seeking nor offering any help. Some will make their way through quickly; others will take longer. A few may never find their way out.

We will all take different paths through the forest, and experience the forest in our own unique way, but most of us will get through. Likewise, each of us will find his or her own way to heal from grief. Our stories may be similar, but we need to understand that our journey may not look like that of our neighbour. Avoid the temptation to compare.

"When will it stop hurting?"

This is my path through the forest of grief.

Monday, March 19, 2018

Eleven days since Crystle passed. Only two days after the celebration of life we held in her memory. We celebrated Crystle's life as we acknowledged her death. Over 150 people came from far and wide. It was, in some strange way, cathartic for me to feel the love of friends and family. A love they had for Crystle, but also a love they were pouring out on me. I woke up that first morning, alone, in our home. It was about 9 a.m. Sleep was still elusive since Crystle passed. I lay there, my mind racing, wondering what I could do to make things different. The same process I had been repeating every morning since Crystle passed over a week ago. At some point, often fifteen or twenty minutes into my thoughts, as if hit by a lightning bolt, I would snap to the realization, again, that she was gone. There was no changing the fact that she was gone. It was as if I had to convince myself of that reality every day. Then I would berate myself for being stuck in this loop and slip into a feeling of hopelessness.

As I got out of bed, my body ached, everywhere, inside and out. My arms and shoulders ached, but not the ache you feel when you have exercised muscles you haven't used in some time. No, this ache seemed to come from the depths of my bones and emanate outward to my muscles and organs. Did my skin ache, too? Was that even possible? For it felt like even my skin was aching, as if in some sort of concert with every fibre in my body. My chest felt tight, but I somehow knew this was just my grief and not the sign of a heart attack. Or at least, that is what I told myself. The truth is, if I had dropped dead of a heart attack at that moment in time, I think I would have been happy. In hindsight, a selfish attitude.

Taking one simple step was laborious. It felt like carrying a heavy weight on my back. I walked hunched over, each step very deliberate, as if I were not careful, I may fall. I pulled on the same pair of jeans I had been wearing all week. The same socks. I did shower, but not every day, once I was alone.

I knew I had asked our children, now adults and both living away from our home, to leave me alone. I was grateful they heeded my request but a small part of me hoped they might break my rules. Regardless, I needed to face being alone, alone. Once downstairs I was running on an autopilot routine. Coffee was first. I wasn't hungry so I didn't eat. As I stood looking into the nothingness, my coffee grew cold. Then I would plunk down on "the bus." The bus is a red leather loveseat in our kitchen. Crystle and I gave it that name because we spent hours on that couch, both looking straight ahead as if we were sitting on a bus together.

Once I sat down, I would finally take a drink of coffee. I remember thinking to myself that death was now welcome. I no longer feared death. I could not find any reason to live. Yes, selfish, I realize, but that was where I was at in those early days of grief. I wrote repeatedly in my journal for those first few days that I could see no reason to carry on with life. Suicide crossed my mind. I am not ashamed of those thoughts, but I am glad I dismissed that notion rather quickly. Somewhere deep inside, even though I had not given it much thought, I knew I needed to be here for our family. That was perhaps the first ray of sunlight into my dark forest. I had a purpose for living tomorrow, and the next day. Our children needed me to be here.

I was filled with negative emotions. I spoke briefly of these emotions in the introduction and I will share more about those emotions more deeply in their own chapter, but for now, suffice to say I was full of anger, jealousy, and guilt. I was unhappy and I didn't see why anyone else had the right to be happy. I didn't want anyone to be happy.

Eventually I would fall asleep on the bus. Sleep was my best friend in these early days.

Tuesday, March 20, 2018

The second day of my first days alone. I was forced to shower and get cleaned up. I had to meet with the funeral director to make final payment and, more importantly, pick up the urn with Crystle's ashes. I didn't mind being alone but being alone with the thought of never seeing Crystle again broke me. I wondered if I might be *lucky* enough fall victim to broken heart syndrome. I actually looked it up on the Internet to find that it is a real medical condition often caused by stress which enlarges one of the heart's chambers and results in heart failure. Alas, I had to remember my family. I should not be wishing such things on my family or myself.

When I returned from the funeral home, I cleaned off our dresser, which faced my side of the bed. I began to create my shrine to Crystle. The urn with her ashes in the middle. Dried roses from her celebration of life scattered around. Pictures: a close-up of her, a wonderful picture of her on our wedding day, and a picture of the two of us on our wedding day. In that second picture she is looking at me with an expression that seems to say, "Okay boy, let's go live life!" Mementos, like bracelets and jewellery were scattered across the dresser. I had already written a few love letters and placed them in my shrine. There was a statue of a couple—I always thought it showed the struggle of relationships, yet at the same time the intimacy of a loving relationship. I remember when we purchased it. Crystle was never as fond of that statue as was I, but now it seemed to represent us more than ever. My most cherished possession is Crystle's wedding band. As if she knew what was coming, Crystle had removed all her rings at some point early in her illness. I had not noticed. But she left her wedding band on her ring finger. With the swelling from steroids, I was unable to remove her wedding ring in her final days. I had to cut the ring to remove it from her finger. It was the day before she passed when I finally removed it. Sometimes it makes me shudder, wondering if somehow she had taken this act as her time to go. Now I wear her ring on a chain around my neck every day.

When the shrine was complete, I sat and cried. But it felt good and I embraced the tears as I remembered my beautiful wife. I was shedding these tears on my terms. My shrine gave me comfort at night. I have lit a candle every night when I am home, and it brings me great peace. A light for her soul to find her way to me.

Evenings were the most difficult in these early days. It was the time of day when we were almost certainly together. If we were apart, there would be texts and phone calls in the evening. Now, my phone was silent. And when I got into bed, it was empty on her side. I would sigh again as I faced the reality that she would never climb into that side of our bed again.

Friday, March 23, 2018

By the end of the week, each day had come and gone in much the same manner. I was not eating well. I was not getting out of the house unless absolutely necessary. I realized that I had to make changes, or I would be stuck in grief forever.

"Little goals," I wrote in my journal on that first Friday. I needed to establish a routine and set goals for each day.

The goals for each day were few and simple. On that first Friday I had three goals: clean the upstairs bathroom, vacuum upstairs, wash the sheets on my bed. I still have the paper on which I had written that first list, with the check marks beside each task as it was completed. It seems simple but creating and achieving those three tasks that day was a big step forward, as if I had begun a plan to get through the forest instead of just walking aimlessly.

Exercise was the next routine I established. I had ballooned up to the heaviest I had ever weighed. I knew that I needed to lose that weight, and I also needed to be in better physical shape. At first, I determined I was going to run or walk 5 km per day on the treadmill. I absolutely forced myself to do this and it always felt great when I was finished. Gradually, that changed to lifting weights every second day and running a few times each day on the treadmill. Treadmill sessions became shorter and more frequent. I lost thirty pounds on a slow and steady pace over the first year.

I started eating better. Again, routine was my friend. Crystle loved boiled eggs for breakfast so I began to eat two boiled eggs almost every day, occasionally changing it up for an omelet or some other preparation of eggs. Eating eggs for breakfast reminded me of her and I felt good. I love to cook, but in those first weeks I had lost all interest. I forced myself to make good meals and to make new and creative dishes. When I did, I found joy again in cooking. There are many days when I keep it simple now, but that is more a factor of convenience when cooking for one. I make sure I eat healthy and I enjoy being in the kitchen again. Unlike exercise, which I still have to force myself to do, cooking brought a measure of joy back into my life.

Cooking was not the only thing that suffered in those early weeks after Crystle passed. I had enjoyed wine for years and created a nice collection with over 200 bottles, but now I no longer cared about my wine. I cancelled wine club memberships and had no interest visiting local wineries which had long been a favourite pastime. Crystle and I had watched baseball almost as long as we were married. In years gone by a new baseball season was always greatly anticipated by us both. But this year I didn't pay any attention to spring training. I didn't know who was playing for the Jays and didn't care. We also loved and supported the Shaw Festival, having attended almost every play performed over the past decade. As soon as the new season was announced and tickets available, we purchased tickets for our favourite seats at every play. This year, I didn't even know what was playing.

What preoccupied my time now was reading. In fact, reading would become an all-consuming pastime for me. One of the first books I read was *A Grief Observed* by C.S. Lewis. He shares a raw account of his feelings after his wife passed. To be honest, I didn't find his work very helpful because he presented me with little hope.

> "Does grief finally subside into
> boredom tinged by faint nausea?"
> —C.S. Lewis, *A Grief Observed*

I needed hope! I did not need to be told that my life may evolve into boredom and nausea. I found other books that proved a little more helpful in giving me reason to wake up the next day.

Then I had an odd thought—well, odd for an agnostic. "What if Crystle can see my pain?" I wondered. At that moment, I never stopped to consider where the question had come from, for I was a diehard non-believer who felt that all I had of my beautiful wife was her ashes in an urn that sat on the dresser beside my bed.

"I know her heart would break," I wrote in my journal. "She would want me to get past grieving. So, I will do my best for her. I love her so. I miss her so." Reflecting back, I think this thought gave me, not hope, but a reason to defeat grief. A renewed resolve not to be consumed by the sadness of grief.

Saturday, March 24, 2018

Images were flashing through my mind after a night of jagged sleep. First, the image of the shift nurse telling me she was sorry that Crystle has passed. I can never forget looking at the dead body of my beautiful Crystle. I struggled to be near her. Her mouth agape as if capturing her last breath. I did not want to remember her that way. I did not want to feel her lifeless body. My daughter had the strength to meet with the funeral home attendants the following morning when they came to remove her body.

My mind shifted to the painful moments in those last days. Crystle had lost her ability to communicate with us. She understood us, but she could not speak. The look of desperation on her face will forever haunt me. I was unable to help my wife. I despised feeling helpless.

Then my mind flashed to a thousand smiles. Her smile was infectious and her laugh even more so. I sat on the side of my bed in a puddle of tears, heartbroken with my memories, consumed in grief anew.

Saturday's task list was:

- Vacuum main floor
- Clean main floor bathroom
- Thank-you cards
- Finish *A Grief Observed*

I completed my chores and I did finish C.S. Lewis, despite the *cheerful* nature of his writing. I found no solace there. He went on to write of the vicious cycle of grief, telling his readers that on one day you feel you have conquered grief only to find the next day " . . . all the hells of young grief have opened again."

I literally threw the book across the room when I was done. "Why," I wondered aloud, "would anyone facing grief want to read this book?" Granted, it was a wonderful reference for those who had never experienced grief and wanted some idea of what it is like. He certainly confirmed my grief in the pages of his book, if nothing else.

Sunday, March 25, 2018

As the week came to a close, I noticed that evenings were becoming a more peaceful time for me. The shrine that I had created seemed to be bringing me closer to Crystle. I retired to bed early. Of course, it couldn't take the place of Crystle, but sitting with her pictures and memories was bringing me peace. I also knew that once I fell asleep, I would have a reprieve from my grief until I woke the next day.

There is one rather unique event that happened earlier this week, but I am going to share it in the next chapter instead. I mention it here because of its significance in me defeating grief. My first week alone was coming to a close and I still had a long way to go but I had laid the groundwork to start making serious headway on my path through the forest of grief.

The activities were very helpful, but the key to this first week was finding a reason to live, for there were times I did not want to go on. But I found my reason in my family. Our children and grandson. My mother and sister, and Crystle's family, too. And perhaps most important was honouring Crystle by not giving up, just in case she was looking down on me from above.

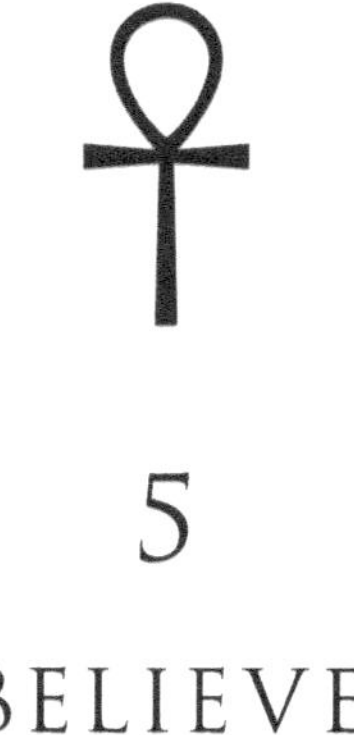

5

BELIEVE

As I entered my second week alone, I was happy that I had made progress the previous week, even if one might consider them baby steps. What happened the second week is undoubtedly the most significant event for me in my journey through grief. Significant in terms of conquering my grief and helping me not just trudge my way through the forest of grief, but race through as if someone has opened a wide path before me.

I found hope!

My new found hope was in believing that Crystle was not just a pile of ashes in an urn, but that her soul lives on and one day we will be reunited.

Look, you cannot fake what you believe. I didn't just wake up one day and tell myself that I was going to believe so I could have hope and see Crystle again one day. It doesn't work that way. At least not in my science-based brain that needs an explanation for everything! You have to find a reason to believe beyond simply wanting to be happier.

I am not talking about finding religion again, but that is not to say religion cannot fill this role. Simply put, religion was not part of this process for me. I am however, going to share the story of my conversion from agnostic to New Age spiritual believer, because that transformation saved me. Maybe saved my life. When I was able to accept that Crystle's soul is still present, I felt like I was in a game of Snakes and Ladders. Do you remember playing that game? If you hit a snake you went backward, but if you hit a ladder you leaped forward. And there is one ladder that catapults you almost halfway across the board in one move. I felt as if I had just hit that ladder and it catapulted me closer to my goal of defeating grief.

I will confess that if I were to relate this story to myself, the guy who was around one year ago as I write these words today, that version of me would have laughed at my new self, quite possibly mocked my new self, and almost certainly passed it off as a fabricated story created by a desperate man. From that perspective, it is difficult for me to share what I am going to share in this chapter because I confess that, at times, I grapple with my own story. Defeating grief is what I seek to share, and my new beliefs are just one part of that larger story. But it is too important to keep to myself.

Let me begin by taking you back to what happened that second week, alone. If you recall at the end of the previous chapter, I shared there was one thing that happened that needed to be divulged in this chapter.

(Before reading further, you may want to take a seat if you are standing—especially if you are an agnostic)

I made an appointment to see a medium. A spiritual medium. For those who may not be certain what that entails, he or she is a person who has the special ability to communicate with souls who have passed. Now, I need you to stop and think about this for a moment: **An agnostic (me), makes an appointment to speak with souls, in whose existence he does not believe.**

The funny thing is, I set up the appointment with the medium as if it was normal practice for me. Having a science-based mind meant I had to have an explanation for myself. It goes like this. When Crystle was still with us, she and I would occasionally have conversations about mediums and the afterlife. I know that she believed strongly in the afterlife. She watched the shows on television that showed mediums communicating with the souls of loved ones. When we discussed the afterlife, and specifically when Crystle would be watching one of these shows on television, it usually ended up with Foghorn Leghorn (me) spouting off about how it was all a scam. It seemed that every time the topic came up, we simply agreed to disagree. Crystle never seemed to feel the need to convince me that the afterlife was real. I cannot help but wonder now if her beliefs made her comfortable that she would be seeing me in the afterlife even if I remained an agnostic to the end of my days. The more I learn, the more I am convinced Crystle always held a strong belief in the spirituality that I hold now. That thought fills me with regret.

It would be a fair question to ask me why I thought to contact a medium. Was it desperation that made me act so out of character? Well, I confess I wondered that myself. But no, I am convinced that Crystle tapped me on the shoulder and told me to reach out to a medium, because she wanted to help me. Please allow me to explain how this was an easy concept for me to accept. For years, Crystle and I have been reading each other's thoughts. We were both convinced of this fact because it happened so frequently. For me, science could support the idea that brainwaves could spill over into each other's consciousness and thoughts could be transferred. We called it mind-to-mind. As an example, I would be sitting beside Crystle and the thought would come to me that we should order pizza for dinner. Before I could get the words out, Crystle would turn to me and ask if we could order pizza for dinner. This happened literally hundreds of times over the years. We never did figure out who was reading the other's mind. We would laugh and be in awe at the same time, no matter how often it happened. So, it is my firm belief that Crystle's soul came to me and generated that thought. I guess that makes me the mind reader.

March 28, 2018

My appointment with the medium is set for Wednesday afternoon at 2 p.m., I arrived at a very normal-looking home in the Niagara region. I was greeted at the door by a very normal-looking woman. I was obviously being influenced by the movies. Perhaps I was expecting a gypsy lady with a witch's hat. I don't know what I was thinking for certain, but I remember thinking to myself that she seemed too normal to be a medium. Then we headed to the basement where I was led into a small room. Now my overactive mind changed direction. "She is not a medium, that is why she looks so normal," I theorized to myself. I had quickly switched gears and was convinced this lady was going to knock me out and harvest my kidneys.

Well, I am very happy to report that this lovely woman was indeed a medium. I still have both of my kidneys—I think? I came to learn that she is also a very compassionate and caring person. I needed both more than I knew. For the next hour and ten minutes Crystle's soul came in to reassure me she that she is still with me, and she will be waiting for me.

I wept and I wept.

For the purposes of this book, I am going to use the name *Joan* for the medium, not her real name.

"I need you to keep your energy up with me," Joan urged as I broke down almost immediately. I didn't have the foggiest idea what she meant by that, but I somehow knew I needed to keep my composure as best I could. Her tone told me she was sincere. This was not the voice of someone irritated with my outbursts of tears; rather, it was a request made out of compassion, letting me know she wanted to do the best for me and that required my being present with her and not lost in my own grief.

The first thing she said to me was that a woman had come forward and identified herself with the word *wife.* One sentence in and I was a sobbing mess. As I composed myself, she went on to say that this woman was very anxious to connect with me because she had come forward in Joan's own personal meditation that day.

It is too much to share everything that happened in that seventy minutes, at least for the purposes of this book. But I need to take some time to share how important this meeting was, for I walked away from this session a changed man, never to be the same again.

What amazed me more than the facts Joan gave to me were the mannerisms of Crystle that she captured. When Crystle first came in she joked about her hair being brunette, but she was really grey and Joan told me Crystle pulled her hair back to show grey roots, and then she laughed. That entire picture is so much like Crystle—only her closest confidants would know that hair colour was such a big deal for Crystle, yet something she would openly laugh about. She loved to tease me by telling me brunettes are really more fun that blondes—you see, I had dated a blonde for a brief period before Crystle and I became a forever couple.

In the reading, Joan told me Crystle was showing me thunder and lightning from her hospital room. I told her that there was no thunder and lightning while Crystle was in the hospital. Twice more during the reading, Joan came back to the thunder and lightning. I kept telling her it meant nothing to me. Finally, Joan said, "I don't understand why Crystle keeps showing me thunder and lightning. But it means something so I will leave it with you."

Fast forward to about three months later. I was listening to a recording of the session with Joan. This time I decided to look up weather history. Crystle was in the St. Catharines General Hospital from July 19, 2017 through July 28, 2017. According to the weather history not only did it rain three times while Crystle was in the hospital, but there were severe thunderstorms on July 20, 23 and 26. My jaw fell open!

If you are a doubting Thomas, like me, you would likely say, "Well, she looked up Crystle's time in the hospital." Let me play devil's advocate on that idea. Joan had one piece of information coming into the reading: my name. I didn't tell her who I was looking to connect with. Okay, fine. Let's assume Joan googled my name and found Crystle's obituary. Nowhere in the obituary did it say when Crystle was in the hospital, or even if she was in the hospital. When I realized how significant that piece of information was—and the fact that Joan kept giving me the same information despite my repeated replies that it meant nothing to me—I simply could not refute the evidence that Crystle had been with us that day.

I could go on to share a dozen more facts that Joan shared with me that left me no doubt that Crystle had to be speaking with her. But I hope I have conveyed the gravity of the effect this meeting with Joan had on me as an individual. I don't believe I walked from her home that day; in fact, I am quite sure I floated out.

I made one simple entry in my journal: *Wow! Did Crystle ever come through. Hard not to believe.* My belief was not instantaneous. My old science-based, show-me-the-proof, agnostic ego was battling for its life. But I had something I had not had since the love of my life passed away.

I had hope!

When I arrived home, I noticed that the knot that had been tied in my stomach the past two weeks was gone, at least for now. It took a while for it to leave permanently, but this was the first relief I had experienced. I came home and ate everything in sight. I must have eaten 3000 calories. I ate quinoa salad—half of a Costco container, so you know it was not a small amount. Costco does not do small. I downed leftover chicken I had in the fridge. Potato chips and chocolate almond beverage. Cookies. Ice cream. Probably more food than I had eaten in the past five days combined. I cried but these tears did not come from the depths of sorrow, they came from a place in my heart—they came from joy. What was this feeling of joy? Not long ago I wondered if ever I would feel it again.

March 29, 2018

I wrote in my journal today that I had not sighed all morning. I cannot remember the exact timing of when those deep, endless sighs came to a halt, but I do remember how they diminished after meeting with Joan. Today was the season opener for the Toronto Blue Jays. I watched the game— a big step for me. It was difficult watching without Crystle. We had watched so many opening day games over the years that it was somewhat melancholy for me, and to make matters worse the Jays lost at home to the Yankees, 6-1.

I'd like to be able to say that my new-found hope in the belief that Crystle was near me was a rocket ship to joy and bliss. But like anything based on faith, my mind continually challenged me and questioned my new beliefs. It is so much easier to be an agnostic, a non-believer. You don't have to do anything to be a successful agnostic.

I began to read everything I could on the afterlife. One of the most compelling books I read was *Proof of Heaven* by Eben Alexander. Eben Alexander is a neurosurgeon who shares the amazing story of his near-death experience (NDE). He received his medical training at Duke University and went on to teach at a number of schools, including Harvard Medical. He was working at the University of Virginia as a neurosurgeon when he was stricken with a previously unknown strain of meningitis that attacked his neocortex. He shares his story of going to heaven while his brain was in a medically induced coma. This was the last book Crystle had read. I had known it was about a near-death experience, but typical me—the old me—I dismissed it as nonsense.

As I think back to Crystle's last days before she passed, I have two very distinct memories that were my own experiences with the afterlife, or heaven, or whatever you choose to call it. The first was Crystle reaching out into what appeared to us to be empty space in front of her, as if she was reaching for something or someone. I remember my daughter and I looking at each other in wonderment. I am certain we both had the same thought, that perhaps she was seeing an angel or loved one who had come to be with her and comfort her in her last days. I wanted to believe but at that point I simply was not able to accept the idea of angels.

The second was a more personal experience. Each morning during Crystle's last week I would come downstairs at about 5 a.m. to relieve either one of our children who had been up with her through the night, or a shift nurse. As I sat beside her bed, I would lay my head down and nestle into her side, looking up toward her face. It was dark. When I closed my eyes, I saw two bright lights dancing beside what would have been Crystle's head if my eyes were open. The tighter I closed my eyes, the brighter they seemed to become. At that time, I somehow imagined this was her cancer, taunting me. I swore that I would hunt it down and destroy it. This happened every morning for the last week until she passed. Thinking back now, it sends chills through me, and I cannot help but wonder if this was an image of angels come to comfort Crystle in her last days. I cannot help but chuckle. What did those two angels think when this guy started swearing at them and vowing to kill them? I hope they had a sense of humour, and I may feel better knowing that maybe they had sent me a few heavenly taunts.

I am not looking to convince anyone that my beliefs or any belief system, is a solution for grief. But I do encourage you to find hope in whatever beliefs you have, and in whatever faith you choose to find. If you are like I was, and you have no faith, I simply urge you to keep an open mind. No single event has had a greater impact on my walk through grief than finding hope in my belief that Crystle's soul is with me today and she waits for me in heaven.

If I did not have hope, I would not be writing my story, for I believe I would have nothing to share. I would most likely still be somewhere in that forest looking for a way out and with no idea how to get there.

6

ATTITUDE AND GRATITUDE

Attitude

"Don't Sweat the Small Stuff."

These were the words Crystle wrote in a small inspirational book she gave to one of our friends three decades ago. That same friend sent me a card sharing with me how much Crystle's friendship and encouragement had meant to her all those years before. Crystle lived her own life by those words. Her attitude was always positive. Her glass was always half full.

Now, what is truly amazing is that in over thirty-six years of marriage her attitude never seemed to wear off on to me. I consider myself a very optimistic person, but oh!—I WOULD sweat the small stuff. Whenever Crystle and I had a spat, I can assure you it was almost always because I was sweating the small stuff. I recall one situation that has remained with me for decades, emblazoned in my mind as clearly as if it happened yesterday. I am a little competitive. Okay, I confess I am—or at least I used to be—very competitive. That spilled over into my driving (head bowed in shame). We were driving up the Don Valley Parkway one afternoon and I cannot tell you for certain what the offending driver may have done to stir up my ire, but I remember my reaction. I hit the gas, swerved in and out of traffic and was soon tailgating my victim. I will never forget the look on Crystle's face. I don't know how to describe her look, that showed anger, fear, and disappointment (in me), all at the same time. Any sane man would have stopped at that moment, but not me. I needed to teach this driver a lesson. At this point the incident has become an emotional vortex drawing me further into its murky shadows. To stop now would have somehow made me less of a man.

"Stop it!" shouted Crystle, in a voice that elicited all the emotions that were on her face. I relented. But now I turned my anger on her. The reality was I was angry with myself, but being the chivalrous man (NOT), that I was back then, I decided to lay the blame on Crystle.

Truly, when I think back on moments like these, I know that I am one of the luckiest men alive to have been blessed with the love that Crystle gave so freely—even when I was a bonified jerk!

I am happy to say that Crystle did have an effect on me over our years together. I have mellowed, but I never truly was able to *not sweat the small stuff*. These little things seemed to loom even larger with her passing. Words people would use became a big deal to me. I would get all knotted up inside and harbour frustration and resentment. But what I eventually learned was that letting the words of others, who really meant nothing more than to try to offer words of comfort to me, letting those words make me angry was going to do me no good. I have to wonder if perhaps Crystle wasn't whispering in my ear each time I felt myself heat up, imploring me to let go of the small stuff.

Let me share a few of the phrases that made me sweat the small stuff. I still don't like them, but looking back, I have to say that for me to have gotten angry at friends and family for speaking such words is humbling.

"The new normal"

I was not interested in thinking about a *new normal*, much less discussing what that might look like. Certainly, just after Crystle passed, all I wanted was to wake up from this awful dream. I didn't want a new normal, I wanted the old normal. And if I could not have the old normal, I surely did not want to think about what a new normal might be like. Even today, I dislike like this term. I know it is reality—trust me, I am well aware of that fact. I have no choice but to walk in a new normal. But please, just use another term if you meet me on the street. And take comfort in knowing that It is my issue, not yours, if you do happen to utter these words and see me wince a little.

"Moving on"

Like the previous expression, *moving on* could be considered similar words of encouragement. But *moving on* bothered me in a different way. To me it was as if I was being told to leave Crystle behind. I know that was never the intended meaning from the well-wishers who unknowingly ignited my ire, but that is how I internalized those words. I am still not ready to leave Crystle behind and may never be ready to let her go. Some may say that I am not being realistic. I don't view it that way. Crystle is still a very real part of my life. I am moving on with my life, but I am not going without Crystle. Nora McInerny uses a term in her TED Talk that I like: she says she is "moving forward" with her life. Like me, she is not moving forward without her loved ones, including a spouse, who have passed.

"Sympathy"

I would actually throw cards in the garbage if they used the word *sympathy*. Not a proud moment for me. Silly semantics on my part. I didn't want sympathy, I wanted empathy and hugs and support. I decided to blame the greeting card industry, not the sender. "Let it go, Glenn," I remind myself.

"It must be so difficult"

Everyone meant well when they would greet me and say, "It must be so difficult." There were times when I wanted to scream and say, "Ya think?" Friends were truly trying to be compassionate and I chose, in those early days, to become angry. Never outwardly; at least, I hope not.

But there was a catharsis for me. I used to believe in coincidences. Now I believe everything happens for a reason. I saw an interview that made me realize how silly I was being. A gift from heaven to help me change my ways. A very prominent business leader had recently lost a spouse and was being interviewed. When the interviewer asked the person how they were doing, the reply was something akin to this, and I am paraphrasing: "How am I doing **now**. That is what you should be asking me, not how am I doing. I just lost (my spouse) . . . How do you think I am doing?"

I sat in stunned silence. Because of one little word missing, this person had just berated the interviewer, publicly. I wasn't judging them, no. I was too busy seeing myself in their behaviour. And I did not like what I was feeling. It helped me understand that I needed to look beyond the words and focus on the intentions. Once I did, pent-up emotions melted away. It helped me become less judgmental, more accepting of compassion. And in turn, I was able to become more compassionate.

It was like a smoker quitting cold turkey. Now when I hear these words spoken, I smile and warmly accept that the person speaking is simply trying to walk with me the best way they know how. The words still bother me, but I let them wash over me and I focus on the loving intent behind them. This change in my attitude had a huge impact on my journey through grief. I was no longer wasting energy getting upset over the words people used, and that was energy I could use to battle the pangs of grief. The amazing part of this is that it felt really good. Suddenly, instead of being wrapped up in anger and frustration, I was open to accepting the love that was being sent my way.

Gratitude

Once I stopped being so judgmental of the words people were using in their sincere attempts to comfort me, I began to drop my judgment of others in all areas. I had never realized before how much energy it consumes for us to get upset at the actions of others. My grandfather used to say, "Don't let the actions of others determine your reaction." His words ring so true to me today in an entirely new way.

So, I took it one step further. I adopted an *attitude of gratitude.* I began a daily routine whereby I started and ended each day quietly reflecting on things I was thankful for in my life. I was surprised at how easily gratitude flowed into my mind. Obvious things like being thankful for family and friends. Harley, my dog, who always greets me with her very loud hello and wagging tail, even at fifteen years old. At night she snuggles close to me and has provided me the comfort of a loving pet. Just hearing her breathe as she sleeps fills me with gratitude. But I began to be grateful for little things, too, like a good cup of coffee or a smile from a stranger.

I found that as I sat for just a few moments and reflected on what I was grateful for, my energy lifted. It felt like my heart was growing and might pop out of my chest. Once I started this routine, it stopped being a routine. I look forward to my quiet moments at the beginning and end of each day where I receive the gift of warm fuzzies, just by focusing on what I am grateful for in my life at that moment.

As I read more in my search for help along my journey through grief, I came across a term that is very much in vogue today: *mindfulness.* There are entire books on mindfulness, but my very simple assessment of mindfulness is living the attitude of gratitude every moment of every day. Our lives are hectic and complex. The stress of careers, mortgages, raising a family all take their toll on each of us. The idea of mindfulness, at least as I perceive it, is to live in the moment. And to live in the moment simply means to be thankful for what is before us right now.

One of my favourite and perhaps most succinct descriptions of mindfulness, whether he intended it that way, is from cartoonist Bill Keane: "Yesterday is history, tomorrow is a mystery, but today is a gift. That is why it is called the present."

Almost thirty years ago we purchased a house in New Brunswick. Crystle and I had decided to move close to my parents while our children were young so my parents could enjoy their grandchildren at that stage of their life. I was the emissary sent to look for a new home. The house I chose was not the right house for us at that point in our lives. It cost us financially to maintain and, ultimately, when we sold it. For decades that mistake lurked in my mind and I would find myself mulling over the decision, reliving the buying and selling of that house. Why? What was the benefit in replaying this part of my life over and over? There was none, is the blunt answer to that question. But that is what we often do to ourselves. We stew over past decisions that we feel were mistakes. Or we worry about what may happen in the future. I am not implying we do not need to plan for the future, but if thoughts of tomorrow so consume us that we cannot enjoy today, then it is time to stop and make some changes.

In my own life, I was so busy working and paying bills and planning for tomorrow that I did not enjoy each day to its fullest. "Tomorrow," I would think, "I will slow down and enjoy life. Tomorrow." Then Crystle was stricken with brain cancer and gone from me in what seemed like a moment. What good did all my worrying about tomorrow do if the love of my life is gone?

I am far from perfect, but I do my best to live each day mindfully. Things creep up on me and I worry about things that may come my way. Or sometimes I find myself trapped in a cycle of regret, thinking about things in the past I may have been able to have done differently. But now my mindset is changed. As soon as I recognize those thoughts creeping into my consciousness, I simply acknowledge them as part of my life, take a deep breath, and look around for things in my life, right at that moment, for which I am grateful. I refuse to let mistakes of the past or the unknowns of tomorrow consume my energy and steal today away from me.

7

JAG: JEALOUSY-ANGER-GUILT

One of the things I had been looking forward to in my life was watching Crystle grow old, and of course, being there with her. There is a country song titled, "Head Over Boots" by Jon Pardi. Two lines from that song say, "Test time and grow old together, rock in our chairs and talk about the weather." I tingled with anticipation every time I heard that song and we danced around the kitchen together, laughing and dreaming of the future that would never come. It may sound a bit strange, but I know Crystle would have been a stunningly beautiful senior citizen. Oh, she would tell you I am looking through rose-coloured glasses. I say phooey. Crystle's beauty shone from the inside out. In my mind, I have a picture of Crystle in her late sixties: she has finally let go of her brunette status and sports a beautiful silver-grey coif in its place. Nails are always done to perfection, and of course, she's always donning age appropriate attire. One of her oft-used expressions was that any clothing or adornments must be age appropriate. Oh, how I miss her!

I now find myself drawn to observing women quite the opposite of what one might expect for a man in his late fifties. My eye is not drawn to younger women, but rather older women in their sixties and seventies. Not lustfully, rather my gaze is wistful. My mind quickly inserts Crystle's face into the picture and I wonder if that is how Crystle would have looked.

Today, I enjoy these memories. I allow myself to linger in those *what-if* moments. Sometimes I cry but most times I smile from ear to ear and get warm feelings as my mind draws a picture of Crystle as a beautiful sixty-something-year-old.

It was not long ago that I would not have been able to enjoy any memory of Crystle. I was consumed by my emotions. This was in the very early stages of my grief, only a few weeks after Crystle had passed. I have mentioned them before, but there are three specific emotions that truly consumed me as I struggled with grief in those early days. They deserve some discussion, or perhaps, my confession: jealousy, anger, and guilt.

Jealousy

Jealousy was an unexpected part of the evolution of my grief. In the first month after Crystle passed I found myself going through a loop of negative emotions. I had never been a jealous person. Oh sure, I definitely had pangs of jealousy at times in my life, but overall, it was not an emotion that I had to battle. At first, I didn't notice the path my emotions were taking because the weight of pure grief was so heavy. It would start with a very innocent event that my mind would blow out of proportion. I wasn't jealous of anybody's car or their beautiful home. I wasn't jealous of the vacations everyone was taking. I was jealous of the people just walking through a store. I was jealous of that couple in the mall. I didn't even care if they looked unhappy— they were still a couple. Everywhere I went I saw couples. Well, duh! Of course, I would see couples in public. But now they were triggering this cascading trio of emotions.

Jealousy was usually the catalyst for this trio of emotions. Then jealousy would quickly give way to anger. My mind would segue into the *Why me?* monologue. Why am I the one walking alone? Why did my wife have to be taken from me? I would let the entire scenario grow and grow and then like all the ingredients of a witch's brew, I would let it just simmer. The result was I became a powder keg. Anger was always just below the surface in those first weeks.

Then the last of this trio of emotions would rear its ugly head—guilt. Why was I being so harsh toward people who certainly did not deserve my wrath, even if they were blissfully unaware of my wrath. This would in turn result in me berating myself for having such thoughts.

What is wrong with you? I would think to myself. Now, I found myself wanting to run up to the same couple I had been jealous of five minutes earlier and ask them to forgive me.

Thankfully, I avoided any personal embarrassment in those early days of grief. At the same time, I simply chose to ignore this cycle of emotions and the fact that jealousy was the instigator. It seemed weak. How could I be jealous?

Anger

Some well-meaning folks told me I had a right to be angry. If only they had understood that I needed no encouragement in my anger, I hope they would have chosen a different piece of advice to give me. It was easy for me to subscribe to that mantra, at least for a while.

I was angry at everything and everyone. There were a number of times when I was on the treadmill and a song would play that sparked a memory, or I might glance at a picture of Crystle smiling back at me . . .

Then, rage.

It often meant I hit the closest thing to me. The result was always the same. I would hurt my hand and the treadmill railing would go unscathed. I was like Pavlov's dog. It took a few times before I began to think better of my outbursts and learn to just be angry without the physical response. Not my finest hours.

I was angry at Crystle's doctors. I replayed the entire seven months over and over. Her medical team had been very quick to prescribe anti-seizure medication when Crystle was not having any serious seizures. And just as quickly her daily dose went from 500 mg per day to 3000 mg per day. Crystle began having seizures and was hospitalized by ambulance twice due to their severity. As her cancer progressed, the seizures became more frequent, often occurring several times daily, although they were not as severe. Why did they prescribe levetiracetam (anti-seizure medication) in such a large dose? And why had I been so willing to follow them blindly? For when Crystle finally began refusing her medications the last few weeks of her life, she never had another seizure. I knew it didn't matter in the end, but I seemed to need to find someone to blame for all this pain, someone with whom I could be angry.

I will never forget the telephone call I had to make to our life insurance company. When the representative answered, I could not get any words to come out of my mouth. I tried in vain to push the lump back down my throat. I burst into tears. Not the first time she had faced that reaction, I suggest. She was very perceptive and quietly said to me, "Take your time." Her kindness helped. When I finally regained my composure and told her why I was calling, she simply contacted our agent to start the process.

Our life insurance company chose to question the claim I filed. Not because they were justified but simply because they could by the letter of the law. The physicians were off the hook, for now. The life adjuster was my new enemy. I recall sending a number of sarcastic emails and then one day I was on the phone with our life agent. I was so enraged I could hear my heart beating in my ears.

That was the breaking point. Something inside me said, "Let it go." It was if for a moment I was standing back as an observer in this event that was playing out in my kitchen as I was speaking on the phone with our agent.

I realized that my anger was a negative emotion that was consuming me, and when I stepped back and took a look at myself, I did not like the angry man I saw.

I wish I could say that I had come to that conclusion on my own. I wish I could say that family and friends guided me to take it easy, but I had so isolated myself in those first weeks after Crystle passed, no one knew what was going on, not even my family. Perhaps my mother noticed, I have never asked her. She must have noticed a drastic change in my tone. She was the only person I spoke with in those early weeks. I talked to her every day. For the first weeks I know I was railing about doctors and insurance companies. I remember the day after my epiphany on anger, and when she asked about the insurance, I remember saying that I had let it go and what would be, would have to be.

I can only conclude divine intervention stepped in and answered my prayers. For in those very early days I was asking for help. I didn't even know what help I needed, I just remember asking God to help me get through this time and find a reason to live again. Yes, I acknowledge I probably didn't know what I was asking of God, but if you are going to ask God for help, be careful, he just might answer your prayers. Mother Theresa is quoted as saying something to the effect of, "I know God trusts me, but sometimes I wish he didn't trust me so much."

I do not mean to imply I have any measure of the love and compassion of Mother Theresa, only to say that God does answer our prayers.

I cannot tell you in good conscience that I never feel the pangs of jealousy or have a moment of anger these days when someone cuts in front of me on the highway. I am still human. I have not been granted any special status. The difference now is that I catch myself almost instantly. I acknowledge my humanness and let the negative emotions go. And I take it one step further: I actually send a blessing to the person who may have caused my anger or jealousy.

Try it. It is amazing. You simply cannot be angry at the same time you are sending someone a blessing. And I can almost guarantee a smile on your face.

There was one more area that fell under anger that needed *letting go*. I came to realize that I had been carrying grudges with me for years. A whole suitcase full. I expect the majority of individuals with whom I had been harbouring these grudges had absolutely no idea that I felt any ill will toward them. As if grief isn't heavy and hard enough, I willingly carried this extra baggage with me. One by one, I took each person out of that suitcase. I thought about what had happened to cause me to carry this grudge for so long. And really, what is a grudge but never-ending anger? So, with each person, I forgave them, sent them a blessing and let go of the grudge.

When the suitcase was empty, I burned it so I could never hold a grudge again.

Guilt

There is another side of guilt I needed to deal with besides the guilt I felt that was attached to my jealousy: guilt about Crystle's death. This is a difficult one. I don't know that it ever fully leaves you, but I have learned to accept it. I have wondered for endless hours why she got cancer. Was there something I could have done? Some early warning sign that I should have seen? Did I give her the proper care? I know I looked after her each day and I am so happy I could be with her to the end. I questioned her medications, but sometimes I wonder if I was too late. If I had pushed back on some of her medication, would she have had a better quality of life in her last days? There were times when I became exasperated with her during her illness. Her cancer, glioblastoma multiforme, changed her in so many ways. She would awaken in the middle of the night and it was a thirty-minute ordeal for her to go pee. Sometimes I would lose my patience, and I instantly felt two inches tall. I asked for her forgiveness, but a childish grin and a blank stare were all that were returned. I don't think she realized I had lost my cool with her. A bittersweet pill to swallow. But still guilt, and a large heaping of it.

The only way I have been able to reconcile these feelings is to know that Crystle has forgiven me for those moments. I know she loves me. I know she is waiting for me.

It was a crucial part of my journey to mitigate the havoc these emotions created in me for the first few weeks and months after Crystle passed.

8

PRAYER ~ MEDITATION ~ MINDFULNESS

If I were making my way through a jungle forest, I would want to have a good complement of tools to help me on my way. I can imagine that in a real jungle my tools would likely be an axe, a compass and a rope. The axe would help me cut away the underbrush and clear a path. A compass would keep me heading in the right direction, ensuring I was not moving in circles but focused on the other edge of the forest. And the rope would be helpful for keeping me out of trouble as I made my way through the jungle. Should I slip into a hole, the rope would help me get out and keep going. I would feel comfortable that my chances of getting to the other side of the forest were greatly enhanced with these three tools. So, too, in making my way through the forest of grief, I needed tools to get to the other side.

Prayer, meditation, and mindfulness. These became the tools to help me through grief. These are the tools that helped me overcome anger and jealousy and guilt.

Prayer

As I began my journey with grief, prayer was the furthest thing from my mind. But prayer became my axe. When I needed help clearing the way, prayer was my tool. It wasn't easy for me at first, having been an agnostic for so many years. I felt almost blasphemous in those early prayers. Who am I to pray and ask for help? I was never opposed to prayer. No, it was worse than that. I was apathetic. If someone wanted to pray, whether it be to bless food or pray at a family event, I was happy to oblige. But inside, for the past two decades, I felt prayers were just empty words going nowhere.

To be honest, there were a few times when my anger with the cancer with which Crystle was dealing made me reject prayer. Cards that came to us offering well wishes and prayers for Crystle were often met with a private sneer from me, chiding God for his deaf ears. How could he ignore the prayers of our families? They were all God-fearing Christians! I am not proud of myself for those moments. Again, maybe confessing is part of my healing, but it is where I was at emotionally and spiritually throughout Crystle's illness and in the early days after her death.

Looking back, I cannot help but chuckle to myself as I recall the progression for me to move back into prayer. After I had my reading with Joan (the medium), I had just one single belief. I thought to myself, "Crystle is still with me in some fashion." And that was all I needed at that point. At least, her soul was with me. I didn't give any thought to what that entailed, *her soul being with me*. I never stopped to ask myself *where* she was. For that first few days, she was just *still with me* and that was all I needed to take my first step into the forest.

The first concepts I formulated were that angels were with me, too, in this little space that contained a physical Glenn and the soul of Crystle. For a little while I was okay with these basic tenets: Crystle and angels are floating in some dimension I cannot see, and someday I will join them. Well, it was not long before my naturally curious mind made me ask questions. Where is she? Is she in heaven? Is there a heaven? And ultimately, I came to that big question, "Is there a God?"

How do you turn that boat around? I mean, how do you go from believer to agnostic and back again? It seemed to me that it should be easier to go from God-fearing to agnostic, as compared to going the other way. What is easier than believing nothing? But this time there was a difference. On my return trip I did not find a God to be feared, with a long list of rules. Instead, I found a God who is pure love. A God who loved me unconditionally. A God who welcomed me as His own, no questions asked.

But my scientific mind struggled. I needed more evidence. I explored through reading books and listening to every spiritual pundit I could find on the Internet. As I mentioned before, one of the first books I read after having trudged my way through a few books on grief was *Proof of Heaven*. Through that book my mind was opened to the possibility of God, an intelligent, loving being who created us. And I remember thinking, "I just want to believe in the angels and our souls." That was all I wanted. Believing in God seemed to be so much work.

I went on to postulate that if I had to start believing in God, it would require *faith*. Faith, that word, for me, was like a bad odour. I remember my face scrunching up. Faith required effort and work. I wondered again if I had become an agnostic because it required so little effort. Like a river following the path of least resistance. But there was no turning back this time. I had discovered a different God, and I really liked Her.

This new God was not a mean, judgmental old dude sitting in the heavens looking to inflict pain and suffering on his children. As I reached out to God, all I received was overwhelming love in return. Here was I, the prodigal son who had turned his back on God for decades, and as I timidly reached out, wondering what retribution and restitution may be awaiting me, I received nothing but love.

You may ask what I mean by receiving love from God. Many will understand, but if you have never received God's love directly into your heart, you are in for an amazing experience. Much like the Canadian television show, *You Gotta Eat Here*, all I can say is, "You gotta eat here." You have to dine at God's table. The first time I prayed to God—post-agnosticism—it was childlike. I cannot tell you the exact words, but I simply reached out to God and thanked him for loving me unconditionally. I thought my heart was going to burst. Tears poured down my face as I felt the love of God pour into my soul.

This was different than anything I had ever experienced or was expecting.

In my previous experience with Christianity I never found this connection with God. Please do not take these words as a judgement on Christianity, but it simply did not work for me. I know Christianity provides hope and comfort for millions and I would never suggest that Christians are on the wrong path or that they abandon their faith as long as they feel God's love. I support all religions, even though I follow none.

My faith is decidedly New Age. I don't want to go deep into my beliefs because I don't feel it is pertinent to anyone following my journey through grief to understand all the nuances of my beliefs. In fact, to be truthful, I am still defining my beliefs and who God is and how I relate to Him/Her. I believe that having a spiritual community is very important, but I also believe a relationship with God is very personal. I will determine how I relate to God, and how I may choose to worship and talk with God.

For me, as a Christian, prayer had become a routine. It was something I felt I had to do when I got up in the morning and before I went to bed at night. It became another chore not much different than brushing my teeth twice a day. I didn't enjoy myself. It was a ritual I had been taught: invocation, praise, worship, forgiveness, thanks, and supplication. I remember going through all these in my mind and over time it became like a race—how fast could I get through all the parts of prayer. It seemed I just wanted to check the box on that spiritual chore.

Today, prayer is much different. I pray when I feel the need. Some days I do not pray. I enjoy myself every time I pray because I truly want to be there with God. There is no format. Sometimes I focus on gratitude and thanks. Sometimes I pray for others and ask God to work through me as I send love and energy to others. I seldom ask God for anything because I believe that God knows what I need, and He will provide. If I ask for anything for myself, it is for little things. You would be amazed how many times I have breathed a prayer asking Archangel Michael to get the guy behind me to stop tailgating because I am still working on my anger management. And the car backs off!

I ask God to show me the way for my life. What should I be doing with my remaining time here on Earth, because my old vocation doesn't make my heart sing anymore—maybe it never did! I am following a path that my previous self could not have tolerated. I am not thinking too far ahead and doing the best I can to listen to the direction I am given. This book, I believe, is what I have been asked to do at this particular time in my life.

It does not matter, in my opinion, who your God is or that you believe anything that I believe in terms of faith. But I do consider having a belief that we are lovingly created by a higher power who loves us and guides us and wants to communicate with us was a very important piece in my own personal path to defeating grief. I cannot imagine what my life would be like if I remained an agnostic. Prayer was a critical tool in making my way through the forest. It gave me strength and helped me clear obstacles. Prayer is my axe.

Meditation

If you have never meditated, your ideas about meditation are probably much the same as mine were—before I began meditating. When I was first asked to meditate, I had visions of sitting cross-legged on a big purple pillow with incense wafting through the air (cough, cough) and chanting "om" for hours on end. I suppose that can be meditation, but meditation, for me, is much like prayer, in that there is no right way or wrong way to meditate.

Prayer is talking to God; meditation is listening to God.

That is one of the most profound things I have learned regarding meditation. Meditation, for me, is simply being still before God and listening. I started with guided meditations, which simply means following the voice of someone who led me through a meditation. There are as many different approaches as there are practitioners. One says sit up straight with your spine erect; the next tells you to lie down. One insists you exhale through your mouth; the next says it doesn't matter. For me, I simply did what felt right for me. I tried many different practitioners to see what worked for me. I use a wonderful app to help me find my way and learn meditation. The app is called *Insight Timer*, and for me was an easy download from the iTunes store. It is a free app with a ton of content. There is a paid version, but the free content is more than sufficient to get you going.

As I meditated more and more, I found that I preferred to sit quietly with background music or tones. I still follow some guided meditations, but my daily practice is now to sit in silence or with soft music playing. In my morning meditation I have created a secret garden in my mind. I have a very detailed description and it works very well to get me ready for my meditation. I start by walking along a path carved through a heavy thicket. A secret entranceway diverts down another hidden pathway and into my secret garden. The garden is covered in roses. The flowers always change colour. As soon as I enter my garden, I immediately see the colour of the roses in my mind's eye. Sometimes they are all one colour, and other times they are many colours. I am surrounded by flowers on all sides. In the middle is a fountain spraying gently into a reflecting pool. There are four curved, stone benches around the fountain, one in each quadrant: north, east, south and west. When I sit on the benches, I can feel the coolness of the stone from which they are made. It is a peaceful place for me to meditate.

I literally feel the chill of my secret garden as the mist from the fountain drifts toward me. My garden has become a very real place for me. I sit on one of the benches and quiet my mind. Sometimes I sense others sitting with me. Maybe Crystle, or maybe angels. My meditation always finishes with a request for protection during the upcoming day.

My evening meditation is very different. It always involves music or tones and I really focus on letting go and listening. Quieting my mind is the most difficult part of meditation for me. It is easy to become distracted with my thoughts. I am learning to simply acknowledge those thoughts as part of me and my life and simply let them go for now. This helps quiet my mind.

There are times when my day gets hectic and God tells me to sit and meditate. A Bible verse has come to me many times, and I am not sure from where, other than to say directly from God. Psalm 46:10 says, "Be still and know that I am God." When that verse comes into my mind, I will sit, for even just a moment, and quiet myself before God.

Meditation is my compass in the forest. It guides me in my steps and tells me which way to turn. It lets me hear God's voice.

Mindfulness

I have already mentioned mindfulness in the last chapter. And as I said previously, there are entire books on the subject so I will keep my explanation brief. To me, mindfulness is truly living in the moment. Being thankful for what is happening right now. And if things are difficult, I can't ignore that reality, but I look around for something to balance myself. It can be as simple as looking at a blue sky and remembering how Crystle loved to see a deep blue sky. It doesn't make the difficulty go away but it brings a balance, a moment of levity for me. It is living the attitude of gratitude every moment of every day.

Mindfulness is also my tool for keeping emotions in check. I still get angry. But unlike before, when I would let the anger consume me and it would fester inside until I was full of knots and would become enraged, now I am able to quickly catch the anger and stop it before it gets out of control. I acknowledge it and then let it go. For a while I would get very frustrated when I became angry. As if some magic potion or spell should have eradicated anger from my being with my new-found spirituality. Unfortunately, it takes some time to break old habits and feelings, especially ones that have been nurtured for decades.

Mindfulness is my rope on the journey through the forest of grief. I use the rope to keep myself on the path I know I need to be on. If I slip and fall to the side, the rope helps me pull myself from the ditch and carry on.

These are the tools that carried me through my own personal trials and helped me reach the other side of grief on the way to healing.

9

BE SOCIAL

I have a character trait that could be considered both a personality flaw and a gift. I like my own company. No, I don't stand in front of the mirror gazing admiringly at myself. But I am okay being alone. In fact, if being a hermit was a career, I may have looked into that as a profession. As an IT professional working contracts for the past twelve years, I did a lot of work from home. WFH! I loved it. Walking around in T-shirts and old jeans. Working when it was convenient for me but still meeting the demands of the role I was fulfilling. Most of my meetings were remote teleconferences. I thrived. But many of my colleagues were going stir-crazy and often would reach out and ask if we could meet in the office for lunch and some social interaction. It is not that I don't enjoy being with others or that I am anti-social.

Rather, I am just very contented with me as my only company and the idea of being alone.

Being comfortable with aloneness is great if you are an IT guy doing work from home. It's not a great idea if you are grieving. Oh, I thought it was fine. After Crystle's celebration of life, I went a full week with no communication with family and friends, remember? The exception was my mother. When I finally reached out to my children, I realized how much I missed their conversation. My daughter is now a daily call. My son, more irregular, but back to how things were before Crystle became ill. I realized how much I needed them to be a part of my life. They were the first *outsiders* I let back in.

I was a changed person. Even before I embraced the bigger changes that my walk through grief brought to me, I was different. If for no other reason, I was different because I was now a widower. A solo dude. I wasn't sure how to be single with other couples. I didn't want to be with friends, and even some family, because I associated those people with Glenn and Crystle, the couple. My first foray into this realm was lunch with Crystle's sister Shirley and her husband. I did not foresee all that this visit would entail for me. As soon as I walked into their home it hit me like a ton of bricks. We had been in Shirley's home a hundred times—more!—over the past thirty-eight years. I could not recall one time ever being there without Crystle. As we sat to have lunch, it seemed as if all the demons from the realms of hell had gathered beside me and were banging drums and cymbals in my ear, chanting in a taunting voice, "She's gone. She's not here. You're alone." I don't recall much about that day together. Who knows what I may have said—I am too frightened to ask for fear of what tales I may have told. I cannot say, and I have never asked if Shirley knew how much I was struggling to get through lunch that day. I couldn't wait to leave and when I finally got into my car, I burst into tears streaming uncontrollably down my cheeks. I wasn't able to drive until the tears subsided.

I suspect Shirley knew, on some level, how difficult it was for me that day. But she didn't give up. A few weeks later she asked if I would meet them at a restaurant for lunch. That day became a standing joke between the three of us because the restaurant she chose had no tables. It was, for the most part, a takeout bakery. But we ordered our sandwiches and occupied three of the four available stools looking out the window into the parking lot on a dreary, rainy day. It was still difficult to be with them and have no Crystle present. My mind wandered to her laugh. I could hear her laugh and joke with her sister. It was a little easier this time.

Shirley didn't let up. A few weeks later we were headed out again to another local restaurant for lunch. This one had tables and chairs. I will be forever grateful to Shirley for not giving up on me. I would have preferred to just sit at home and be by myself. But at the very least, once a month the three of us explored restaurants throughout the Niagara and Halton regions. Each time it became easier and gradually I came to look forward to our lunches. Shirley never forced me to join them—of course not. But what I realize now is that in getting together repeatedly I established my own relationship with Shirley and Duane. It was a relationship with Glenn, the widower. The single guy. I was becoming okay with that. It opened the way for me to feel comfortable being with other couples who had always been friends with Crystle and me as a couple.

It became an important step for me to be single and be okay with that. I don't know how things would be if Shirley had not continued to nudge me, perhaps without even knowing, toward being Glenn the single guy. I have been asked by friends and family if I would get married again. My first response is to say, "Never say never, but I don't see that happening." That is a very personal decision that each person who loses a spouse has to reconcile in their own mind. No two situations are alike. As time passes, I find myself becoming more and more attached to Crystle and the thought of being with another woman is something that for me I cannot imagine. I know I am in the minority, but that is what is right for me, at least as I write this, one year after Crystle passed.

"You know what I miss most?" a friend asked rhetorically, speaking about her deceased husband.

"Touch. I just want to feel him hold my hand or touch my face."

She is so correct. Science tells us how important touch is to a newborn baby. Even while in the womb, mothers are encouraged to caress their unborn child. Touch transmits love without saying a word.

Touch is an area that, I believe, is unique for those who have lost a spouse. I don't mean to imply that the loss of a child or parent will be any less traumatic. But the touch between spouses is very different than that between any other loved one. I don't mean sensual touch, either. Sensuality is not what I miss most in losing Crystle. It is those intimate moments together that become unspoken habits. For Crystle and me, it was holding hands. We held hands everywhere. Sitting at home. Driving in the car. Walking along the parkway. Meandering through a shopping mall. For me, there can be no replacement for

Crystle's hand in mine. Of course, I hold my grandson's hand when we walk home from the school bus, or if we are out on some adventure together. But it is a very different love.

A warm embrace can only be shared between spouses. I mean more than a hug. Those times when you just linger in the arms of your loved one and time seems to stop. Today, I look for hugs from anyone willing to give them and I enjoy those hugs. They are, dare I say, critical for my survival. But no hug can replace the embrace of a spouse.

Crystle was not prone to snuggling in bed. She wanted her space and when we finally bought a king-size bed her greatest thrill was that she could now have even more space between us when we slept.

"Keep on your own side of the bed, buddy-boy," she used to quip as she tucked herself into bed. It didn't matter that I was banished to my side of the bed, for she was still there beside me. But now climbing into bed alone is something that only one who has lost a spouse must deal with. When I awaken in the middle of the night, I still look over to her side of the bed. Somewhere deep inside me, I am hoping to see the bump under the covers that tells me she is there. But it never happens. I listen for the sound of her breathing, but nothing comes back but silence.

In times like these, we have to look for the beauty in life. I shared almost forty years with Crystle. I have had thousands of kisses, and as many hugs and embraces. We shared private jokes. Held hands for months, if I were to string together all the time we held each other's hand. I cherish those memories. I miss her touch immensely. I understand and support those who choose to find another love. "Never say never," I say. But not today.

I don't seek sympathy; I only seek acceptance for the choice I have made.

Sometimes, when I dream, Crystle shows up and often I get a hug from her. Whether it is my own mind creating that story, or if Crystle's soul knows I need a hug and enters my dream to cheer me up—it doesn't matter to me. When I awaken and remember that brief moment where we embraced, even ever so briefly, I wake up a happy man. I recall one dream where I was walking in a crowd and I suddenly saw Crystle leaning against a fence as the crowd passed by. I went over to her and we hugged and I burst into tears, so happy to see her. Crystle laughed and said, "Well, that is a nice reception." Her voice was loving and sincere. Then she was gone.

My transition from Crystle's guy to just a guy has been a problem for some of my friends and colleagues. Some of the people I worked with and socialized with simply disappeared. At first, I was bothered that friends would walk away from me. But I have come to understand that it is simply part of life. And I am okay with that. I don't know why they stopped connecting with me, but I no longer let it bother me. I hold no ill will toward those who chose to move on with their lives and let our friendship dwindle. In fairness, I never reached out to them, either, so I have shared in the decision that our lives have gone separate ways. Maybe one day, old friendships will be restored, but for now, I have lost a few friends.

My regular lunches with Shirley and Duane have made it easier for me to connect with most of my friends. It will never be quite the same, but I am able to meet with couples socially who were friends with Crystle and Glenn. Except now it's just Glenn, or as I like to refer to myself in those situations, "Crystle's guy."

10

OUT OF THE FOREST

I don't recall the precise moment I stumbled out of the forest of grief. Perhaps I can equate it to breaking through the tree line. Years ago, I hiked a trail in Acadia National Park in Maine. The trail started in dense forest; a picture easy to conjure up if you have ever been to Maine. As I continued on the trail, it made its way up the side of Cadillac Mountain. Slowly the trees began to get thinner as I climbed onward. At last, trees gave way to underbrush and before long I was moving along Cadillac's rock face. I was out of the trees before I noticed they were gone. Defeating grief feels like that: slowly moving out of the dense forest and suddenly you realize the forest is no longer surrounding you. It was very unlike the moment I entered the forest, for back then one step took me from the beautiful meadows of my life into the foreboding darkness of grief.

I defeated grief. Well, at least, I feel like I have defeated grief. I don't say that to boast. To do so would be akin to bragging if I had escaped a burning building while others remain trapped in the inferno. No, I simply say I defeated grief to encourage others. I want to be the one waving a bright light at the edge of the forest for others to see.

"Over here! You can get out of the darkness!"

For me, there were two key aspects of my journey through grief. These are my own personal observations. As I have noted previously, I believe everyone's walk with grief will be unique. While I make no assertion that the path I followed will help anyone overcome grief, I do believe that my first step is one that we all must take. My first step was finding hope. I can't tell you what hope looks like as it will certainly be different for each of us. For me, it was the realization that Crystle was still with me in spirit and I would one day be reunited with her again. This statement is so far from the beliefs I held just one year ago that my ego cries out to add a disclaimer. But I make no apologies for the foundation upon which my hope is built.

"You do not drown simply by plunging into water, you only drown if you stay beneath the surface."

—Paulo Coelho,
Warrior of the Light: A Manual

There is wonderful metaphoric truth in this statement from Paulo Coelho's book, *Warrior of the Light: A Manual.* We only drown in our grief if we stay underwater. It is hope that makes us swim to the surface for air. It is hope that made me take that first step.

I want to be clear. I am not saying your hope needs to be anything like mine or that you need to have a spiritual renaissance. Hope just needs to be something that makes you take that first step. Something that makes you want to swim to the surface. For each of us, just as I experienced, there will be a defining moment when we choose to find hope—and in that hope, we find the strength to begin the journey.

The second key aspect for me to face was forgiveness. I needed to forgive, but I also needed to accept forgiveness. This is something I still battle with today. I needed to forgive others, many of whom would be completely unaware I held them accountable or held any grudge. But more importantly, I needed to forgive myself.

My grandfather was fond of a saying that went something like this: "While you are wringing your hands, your enemy is ringing the bells and dancing." In other words, I am harbouring all these grudges and judgments and it becomes a burden that I carry alone. For my *enemies* have no idea I may be angry with them and carry on happily with their lives. I conjured up all the old grudges, some going back decades. I released them. I simply decided I could not afford to carry them any further. I needed my strength to fend off grief. Then I listed all the people with whom I was angry with over Crystle's death. The list was embarrassingly long! Physicians. Innocent couples who dared hold hands in my presence. The insurance company who seemed heartless. Big Pharma. And yes, even God, who at the time I did not believe existed! If you remember, I put all that anger into an imaginary fire and burned it. I refused to carry the anger any further. It sounds idealistic, but it worked. I refused to carry that emotional baggage one step further in my life. I remember the moment very well. I could physically feel the difference in my body. And I know my mother is still wondering what happened to the raving lunatic that used to be her son, in those early days of grief.

But more important, and for me, far more difficult, was to forgive myself. I was the primary caregiver for Crystle, the love of my life. Did I do all that I could to help her? Did I make the correct decisions? I even struggled with survivor guilt. Why was Crystle taken from this earth? Surely, she had more to give than I? When I laugh and play with our grandson, there are moments when I pause and think to myself, "It just isn't fair that Crystle is not the one to be here enjoying our grandson."

It haunts me to this day. I need to continually forgive myself.

Finding hope gave me the strength to take the first step through grief. Forgiving and accepting forgiveness gave me the strength to carry on after the first step.

The grief I set out to defeat a year ago is a heavy, physically debilitating emotion and all the feelings that are wrapped up with it can easily overwhelm. But it has to be faced and defeated. I use that term intentionally because I believe we have to face grief and defeat it. Time won't make it go away. I met a woman whose husband had passed nine years earlier and she was so overcome with grief she seemed barely able to function. I wept inside for her suffering. We cannot wait grief out. It will never leave us of its own accord.

We may try to run away from grief and escape its terrible clutches. Perhaps we immerse ourselves in work or other activities. We busy ourselves and refuse to look back over our shoulder. Grief will follow us. It will hide around the corner so in that moment when our activity lulls, grief will pounce. Grief will never leave until it is defeated.

When will it stop hurting? When we defeat grief, and that means facing it head-on, whatever that may entail, and for each of us that path may be very different.

I can say from experience grief does go away. I no longer have the oppressive emotions I experienced a year ago. But the hole in your heart from the loss of your loved one is with you forever. Today, mourning has taken over from grief. Mourning is controlled by me; it does not control me like grief did. In mourning I enjoy happy memories and sharing stories with family and friends.

> *"A broken heart is not the same as sadness;*
> *on the contrary, there is an unbelievable*
> *amount of vitality in a broken heart."*
> —Rabbi Scnhuer Zalman

I came across this quote from Rabbi Scnhuer Zalman not long after Crystle passed and it became a mantra for me. I printed it and put it on the wall in the kitchen so I see it first thing in the morning and throughout the day. It helped me understand that my broken heart was merely a sign of being alive. If my heart was not broken, what would my life have been? I cannot deny there is sadness in losing a loved one, for I surely have faced much sadness over the past year. But that sadness is not from my broken heart—no, my broken heart tells me I have been fortunate to have experienced an intense love on this earth that not all of us are able to know.

Yes, perhaps a sigh will sneak up on me occasionally and remind me how terrible grief was to have experienced. But it also tells me how far I have come. I mourn for Crystle every day. I want to do that for her to honour her memory. But now I choose when to mourn, and when to carry on with life.

Mourning is a moment of reflection. I am careful not to dwell on the past too long, for that can be a slippery slope. Sometimes my mourning is stopping for a moment to look at a cherished picture. One night I went to bed and listened to Crystle's favourite songs for about three hours. It wasn't a sad time for me. I welled up with joy as I remembered her singing. Sometimes we danced around the kitchen, neither of us particularly coordinated but we laughed as we moved awkwardly together. Tears still flow at times, but I enjoy those tears for they remind me of the love we have even when I am unable to touch her.

One year ago, I took the first step into grief. I was forced into grief; I wasn't given a choice. I remember my vision, standing at the edge of the forest. Behind me was the lush green meadow of our lives together. When Crystle passed, an invisible hand pushed me into the forest. No one would choose to enter such a dark and ugly place. Once inside, I had a choice. I could choose to sit down and feel sorry for myself, for there was no way back into the meadow. Or I could begin walking. The only way out was to journey through the forest to the other side. There, awaited a renewed life with the desire to live it to the fullest. My life was now without Crystle physically beside me, but it was life!

As I write the final chapter of this book, it is just a few days from being one year since Crystle passed. I calculate that I have missed out on 1,800 kisses and countless hugs from Crystle. While I miss her more than I can put into words, I have learned to be grateful for all that I have in my life and for the beauty around me. I am grateful for all that I have learned. I have changed in many ways. I am not the man I was one year ago. I don't even recognize the person I was back then.

There is one thing I can say for certain about grief: it will change you. Whether you choose to defeat grief or be defeated, you will be changed.

I am over here at the edge of the forest with so many others, waving a light to help you make your way through grief. Look for us. We are your family, friends, and those who have made it through what you are experiencing. You, too, can do this.